MAGIC MONSTERS
Learn About Health

by Jane Belk Moncure
illustrated by Helen Endres

ELGIN, ILLINOIS 60120

Library of Congress Cataloging in Publication Data

Moncure, Jane Belk.
  Magic monsters learn about health.

  (Magic monster series)
  SUMMARY: Magic Monsters demonstrate the results of following a few basic health rules.
  1. Health—Juvenile literature.   2. Nutrition—Juvenile literature.   3. Exercise—Juvenile literature.
  [1. Health.   2. Nutrition.   3. Exercise]   I. Endres, Helen.   II. Title.   III. Series.
  RA777.M66   613   79-24240
  ISBN 0-89565-117-3

Distributed by Childrens Press, 1224 West Van Buren Street, Chicago, Illinois 60607.

© 1980 The Child's World, Inc.
All rights reserved. Printed in U.S.A.

MAGIC MONSTERS
Learn About Health

This is Monster Wobbly-Wibbler.
He is a cake and candy nibbler.
He eats cookies by the ton.
He is too big to hop or run.
Wobbly-Wibbler always eats
too many sugar sweets
   for treats!

Healthy monsters nibble snacks like

carrot sticks and raisin packs,

oranges, apples,

celery too.

Hurrah for Magic Monsters who
know healthy snacks are good for you!

This is Monster Gilly-Glunk.
He rests his head
on an old bunk bed.
He never likes to exercise.
Instead, he closes both his eyes
and dreams of creamy custard pies.

Healthy monsters exercise,
for they are very wise.

They slide,

they hike,

they ride a bike.

They skate,

and swim,

and jump rope too.
Hurrah for Magic
Monsters wise
who take the time
to exercise.

This is Monster Hooley-Hunk.
Most of what he eats is junk.
It may be gooey, chewy, yummy,
but it does not help his monster tummy.
His bones are weak, his muscles flabby.
Junk food makes him cross and crabby.

A healthy monster uses his head
and eats nutritious foods instead.
He eats dairy foods, like milk and cheese;

proteins—meats, eggs, fish, nuts, and peas.

He eats vegetables,
like beans,

tomatoes,

corn,

and yellow
sweet potatoes.

Fruits like grapes and pears are nice.

So are grains like wheat and rice.

Hurrah for this Magic Monster! He'll feel so good after eating a balanced meal.

This is Monster Filly-Flaahs.
She starts the morning with the blahs.
She can hardly bend her knees.
She has no pep or energy
and goes to school so grumpity!

Smart monsters start the day with glee,
for breakfast gives them energy . . .

to throw a ball

or climb a tree.

Smart monsters eat three meals a day,
so they can think and work and play.

This is Monster Droopy-Drap.
He never sleeps nor takes a nap.
He is cranky. He is creepy.
All day long his eyes look sleepy.

Healthy monsters sleep at night
so they can wake up fresh and bright,
full of vigor, vim, and zip,

to climb a mountain, take a trip,

or maybe just to take a dip.

Healthy monsters stay away from

Wobbly-Wibbler,

Gilly-Glunk,

Healthy monsters stay and play
with healthy kids, like you!